LET'S TALK ABOUT IT:

Divorce

FRED ROGERS

PHOTOGRAPHS BY JIM JUDKIS

PAPERSTAR

Penguin Putnam Books for Young Readers

Special thanks to Hedda Bluestone Sharapan for research and development, Barry Head, and all of the colleagues and friends who gave us professional guidance or shared some of their most personal thoughts and experiences with us.

Special thanks also to the parents and children who graciously agreed to appear in the photographs. For some of them, divorce is part of their lives, and we are especially grateful to them because we understand how difficult it may have been for them to relive some of their feelings and experiences for the camera. To those families who helped us but are not directly affected by divorce, we also extend our sincere thanks. We're grateful for the time and energy everyone donated to this project.

Knowing that there are people who understand the need for this book and who were willing to participate was reassuring to us as we did our work.

A PaperStar Book, published in 1998 by Penguin Putnam Books for Young Readers, 345 Hudson Street New York, NY 10014. PaperStar is a registered trademark of The Putnam Berkley Group, Inc. The PaperStar logo is a trademark of The Putnam Berkley Group, Inc. Originally published in 1996 by G. P. Putnam's Sons.
Published simultaneously in Canada
Manufactured in China
Project Director: Margy Whitmer.
Designed by Jackie Shuman and Donna Mark.
Text set in Korinna.
Library of Congress Cataloging-in-Publication Data
Rogers, Fred. Let's talk about it. Divorce / Fred Rogers; photographs by Jim Judkis. p. cm. 1. Divorce—United States— Juvenile literature. 2. Children of divorced parents—United States —Juvenile literature. I. Judkis, Jim, ill. II. Title. HQ834.R618 1994 306.89—dc20 94-2312 CIP AC
ISBN 0-698-11670-4
7 9 10 8 6

Most people want to have a perfect life for themselves and their children. But when we have to go through hard times, it's possible to grow stronger than we ever were before. Divorce is a very hard time for families . . . a sad and painful time. But it can be managed, and both parents and children can grow by helping each other through it.

As with most complicated and emotional things in life, there are no simple answers when it comes to helping children deal with divorce. Each family is different, each parent is different, and so is each child. The best we can give our children is the right to feel . . . the right to feel angry . . . the right to feel pain.

You, of course, know your child best, so I hope you will adapt the ideas in this book for him or her. I hope the pictures and the text will inspire you and your child to relate your own stories which are unique to your family. That's why we call this series of books "Let's Talk About It." It's an invitation to you and your child to take what we offer and talk about it in a way that feels right for you.

"Let's Talk About It" is also a way of saying that when we share our uncertainties (even about difficult things) with people who care about us, we often find that our feelings can be much more manageable. Even when there aren't answers, it can help just to know that the people we love care about our questions and the feelings that go along with them.

That's what a family really is—people who care about each other deep inside: honest and forgiving. When it comes to growing into a healthy human being, it will always be love that counts the most. Even though a mother and father are no longer living together, they can still love their children and give them the secure feeling that comes from being a part of a caring family.

Fred Rogers

Every child needs a family.

Whether your family
is big or small, you
need a family to help
you feel safe,

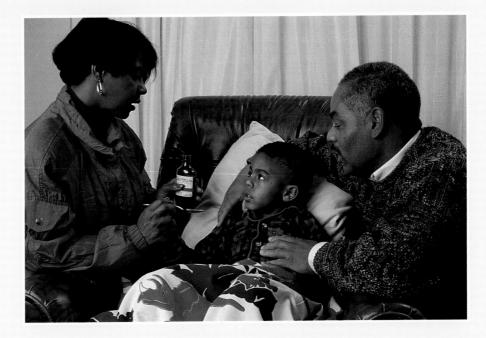

to give you food, to take care of you,

and—to give you love.

Even when parents get divorced, they know their children need food and care and love.

A lot of upsetting changes can happen in a family when there's a divorce. The *biggest* change is that the mother and father live in different places.

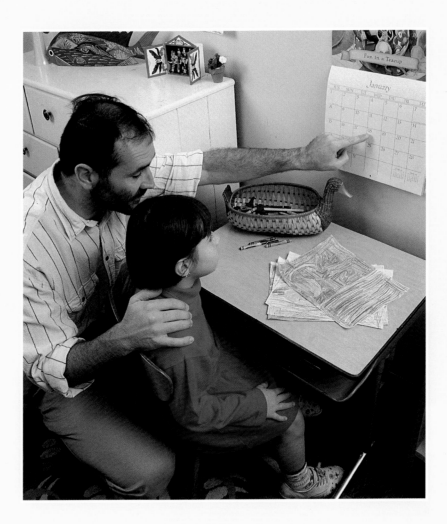

If your mom and dad are getting divorced, you might wonder where you will live, who will take care of you, when you will be with your mom, or when you will be with your dad. It can help to remember that you can always ask the people you love about what will change. . .and what will stay the same.

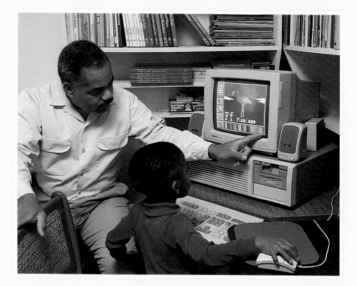

Some things *will* stay the same, even with a divorce. Your mother will always be your mother. . .and your father will always be your father.

But it can be hard when your mom and dad live in different places, especially when you love both of them. Sometimes you might not want to leave your mom to be with your dad, and sometimes you might not want to leave your dad to be with your mom.

And when you have a good time with one parent, you might wonder if it's okay to tell the other parent.

It can help to know it's all right to have lots of feelings about both your mom and your dad.

Sometimes children wonder if the divorce is their fault. They might worry that they made their mom or dad mad enough to go away. There can be many reasons why your mom and dad don't want to live together, but their divorce is *not your fault*. A divorce is about grownup problems and *only* grownup problems.

Nothing you did made your mom and dad get divorced. (It can help to hear that over and over.) And there's nothing you can do to make your mom and dad get married to each other again. Lots of children wish for that, but wishing doesn't make things happen—not bad things *or* good things.

When your parents get divorced, you can have many different feelings. You might feel sad. You might feel angry.

There may be times when you feel like crying.

Sometimes you might want to be alone.

Other times you might want to be close to someone you love. . .

or share your feelings with someone else whose parents are divorced.

Adults can have their own sad and angry feelings about the divorce. You might think there's a way you can make your parents stop feeling upset, and it can help them to know you still love them. But no matter what you do, there are many things that grownups have to work out for themselves.

It can be a hard time for the whole family, but there are some things that can help. Talking about your feelings can help.

So can drawing pictures,

pounding some clay,

going to a special place of your own,

or playing with friends. It really *is* okay for you to have some fun and not think about the divorce all the time.

Many children find that when they get used to the changes, some of the hard feelings about the divorce go away.

Even though some things about your life are different because of the divorce, the most important thing of all stays the same:

You still have a family that loves you. . .a family that needs your love.

Knowing that can give you a very good feeling.